THE ESSENTIAL COLLECTION

SCHUBERT

GOLD

Published by
Chester Music Limited
14-15 Berners Street, London W1T 3LJ, UK.

Exclusive Distributors:
Music Sales Limited
Distribution Centre, Newmarket Road, Bury St Edmunds, Suffolk IP33 3YB, UK.
Music Sales Corporation
180 Madison Avenue, 24th Floor, New York NY 10016, USA.
Music Sales Pty Limited
Units 3-4, 17 Willfox Street, Condell Park, NSW 2200, Australia.

Order No. CH80146
ISBN 978-1-78038-748-2
This book © Copyright 2013 Chester Music.

Music engraved by Camden Music.
Compiled by Quentin Thomas.
CD Project Manager: Ruth Power.
CD recorded and produced by Mutual Chord Studio, Guangzhou, China.

Previously published as Book Only Edition CH67903.

Book printed and CD manufactured in the EU.

www.musicsales.com

CHESTER MUSIC
part of The Music Sales Group

London / New York / Paris / Sydney / Copenhagen / Berlin / Madrid / Hong Kong / Tokyo

Agnus Dei
(from Mass in G)

Composed by Franz Peter Schubert

Arranged by Quentin Thomas

Lento (♩ = 72)

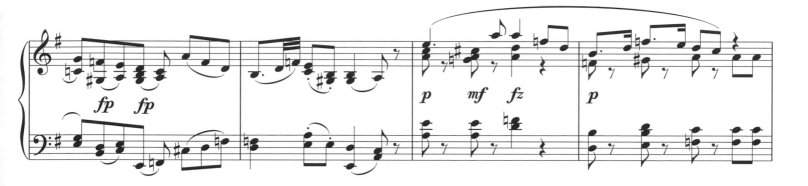

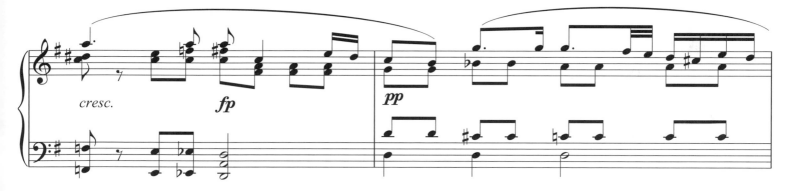

Andante in C major

Composed by Franz Peter Schubert

Andante

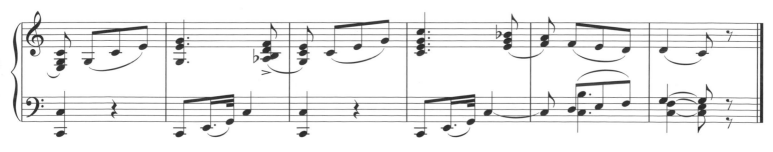

Ave Maria

Composed by Franz Peter Schubert

Arranged by Quentin Thomas

Moderato

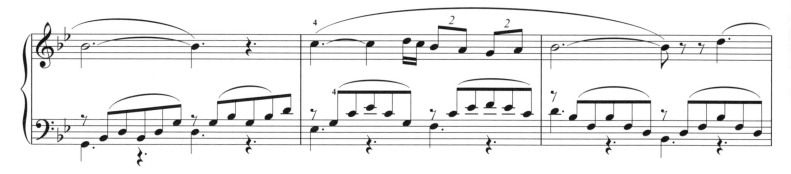

A tempo

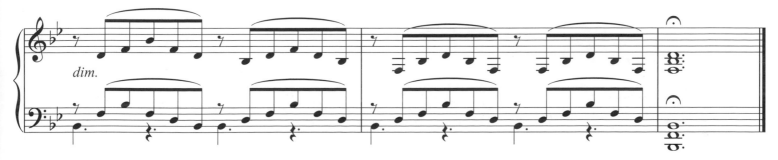

Ballet Music
(from Rosamunde)

Composed by Franz Peter Schubert

Allegretto moderato

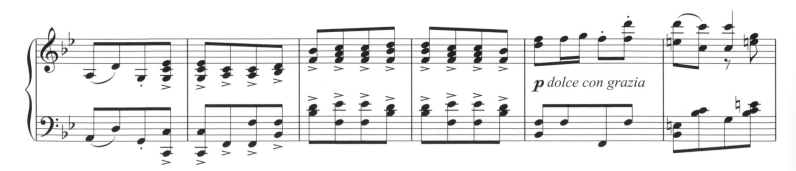

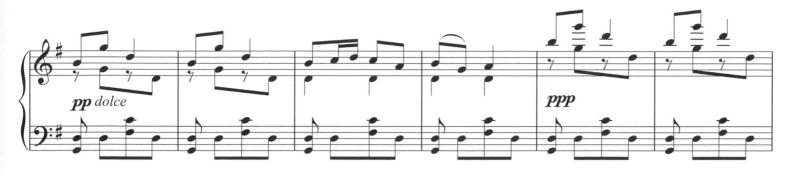

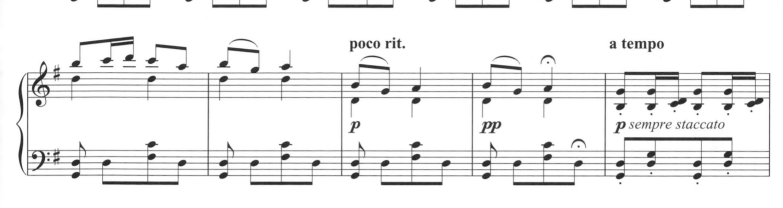

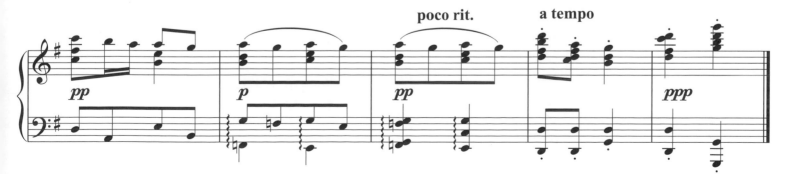

Dances 'First Waltzes'
(Op.9, D.365: No.1, 2 & 3)

Composed by Franz Peter Schubert

No.1

Melancholy Waltz

No.2

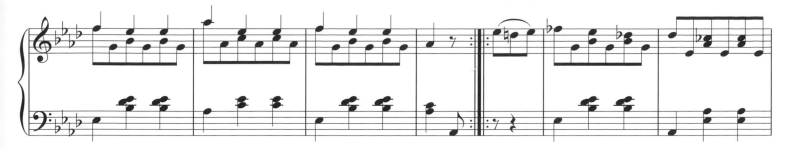

No.3

Diabelli Variation
(Variation on a waltz by Antonio Diabelli)

Composed by Franz Peter Schubert

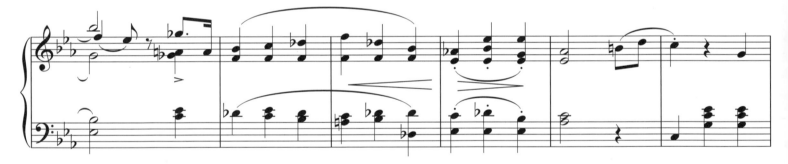

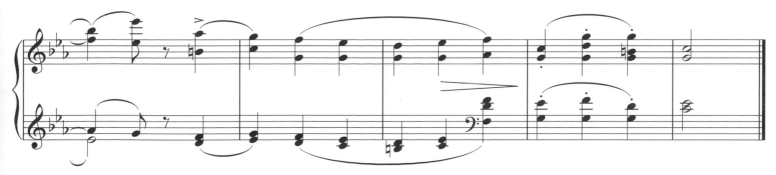

Entr'acte
(from Rosamunde)

Composed by Franz Peter Schubert

Andantino

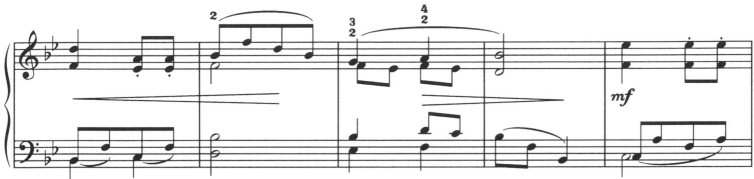

Gute Nacht
(from Winterreise)

Composed by Franz Peter Schubert

Arranged by Quentin Thomas

Moderato

un poco rit.   a tempo   rall.

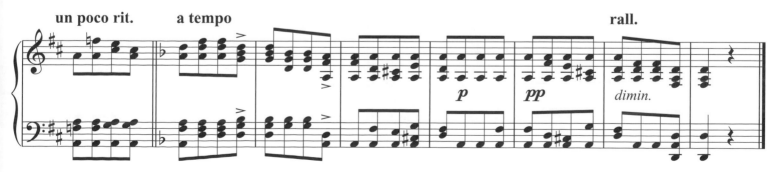

Huttenbrenner Variations

(Variations on a theme by Anselm Hutternbrenner:
Theme and Variations No.1, 2, 8 & 9)

Composed by Franz Peter Schubert

THEMA

Andantino

VAR. I

VAR. II

VAR. VIII

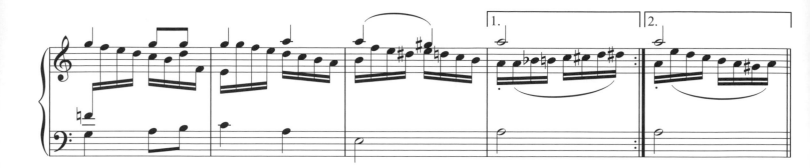

VAR. IX

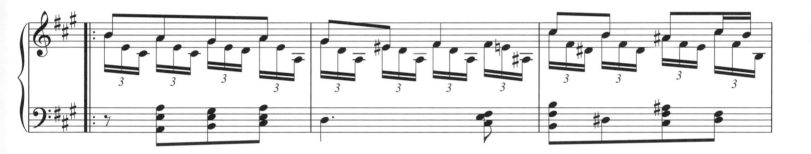

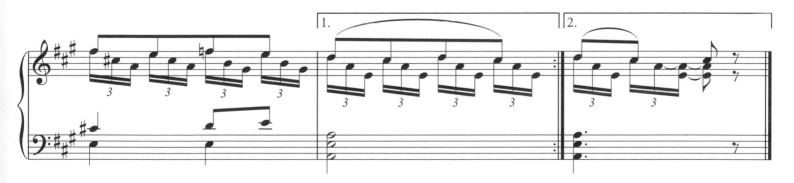

Impromptu No.2 in A♭ major (excerpt)
(Op.142)

Composed by Franz Peter Schubert

Impromptu No.3 in B♭ major (excerpt)
(Op.142: Theme and Variations I & II)
Composed by Franz Peter Schubert

THEMA
Andante

VAR. I. *legato*

VAR. II.

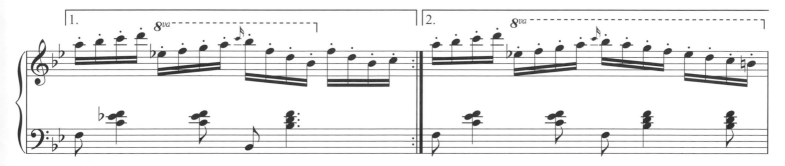

Impromptu No.3 in G♭ major
(Op.90)

Composed by Franz Peter Schubert

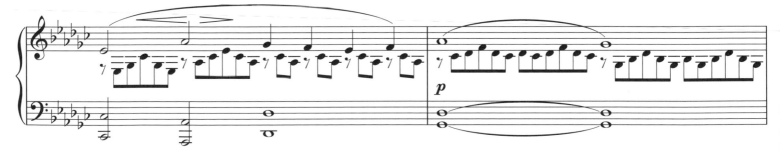

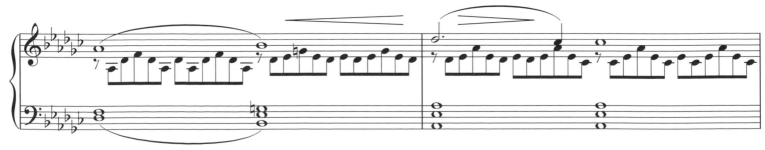

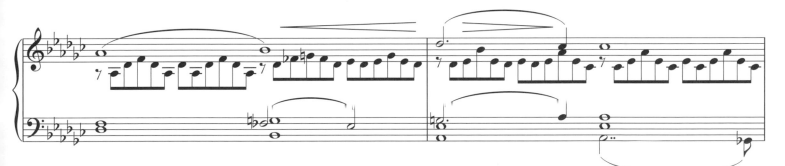

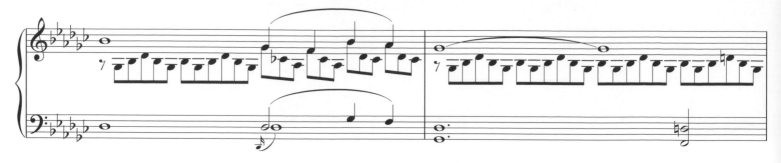

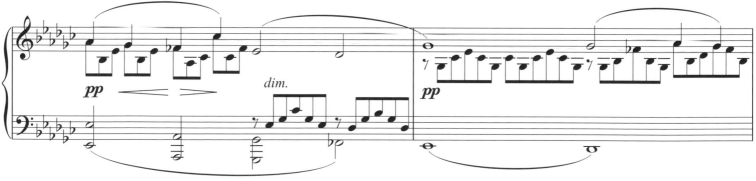

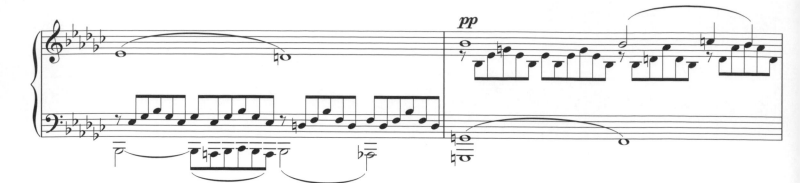

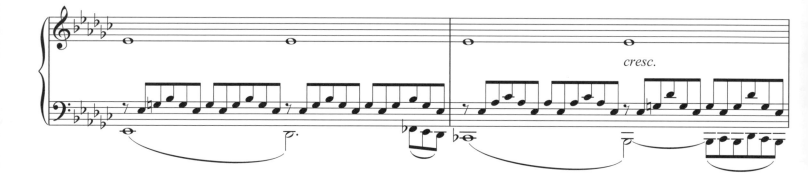

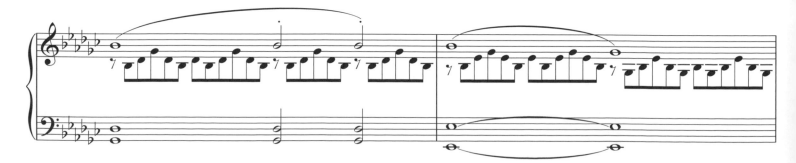

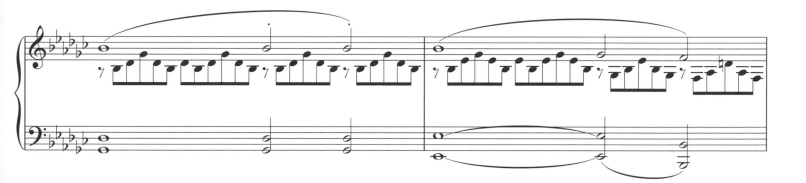

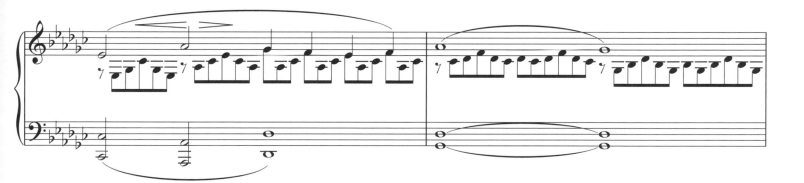

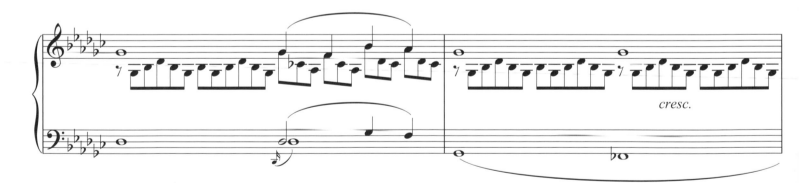

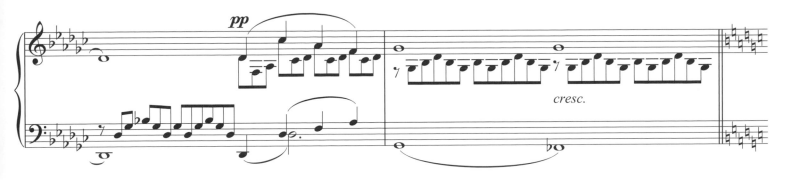

Litaney

Composed by Franz Peter Schubert

Arranged by Quentin Thomas

Adagio religioso

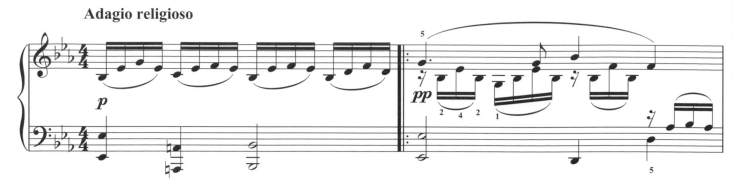

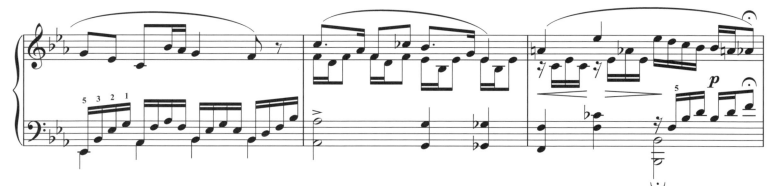

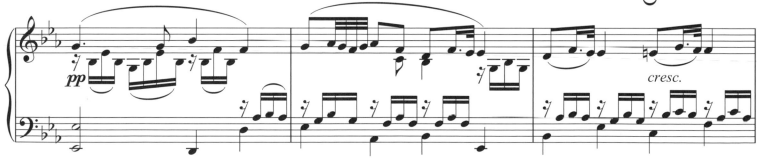

The Lord Is My Shepherd

Composed by Franz Peter Schubert

Arranged by Quentin Thomas

Adagio

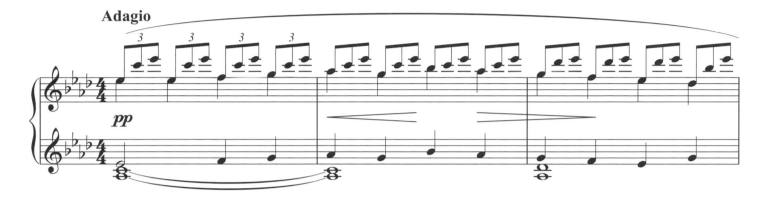

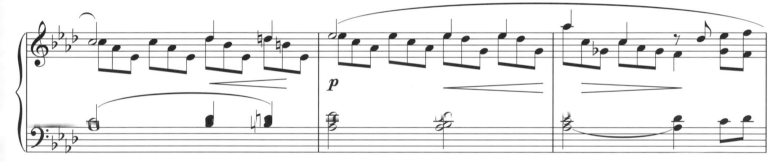

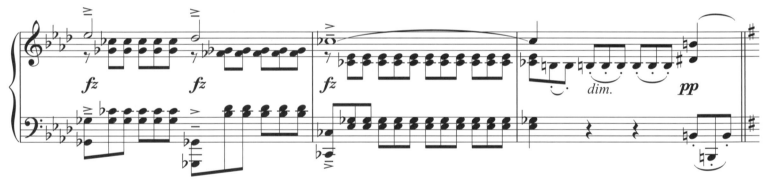

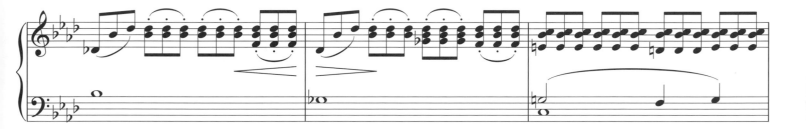

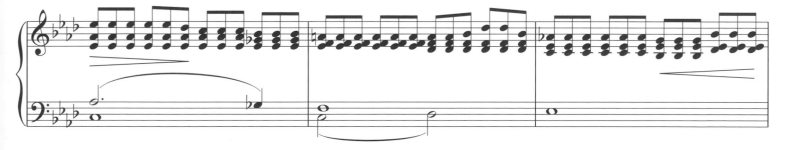

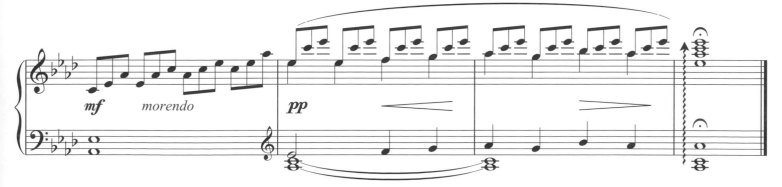

Marche Militaire

Composed by Franz Peter Schubert

Allegro vivace

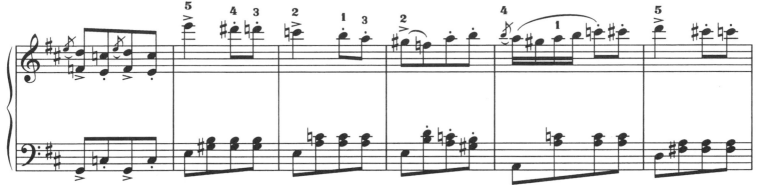

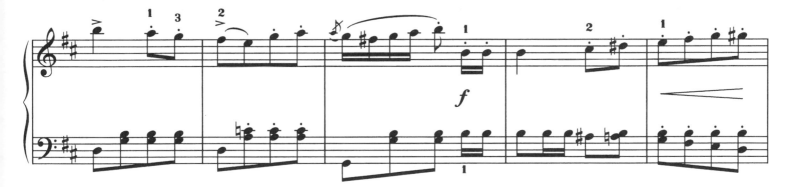

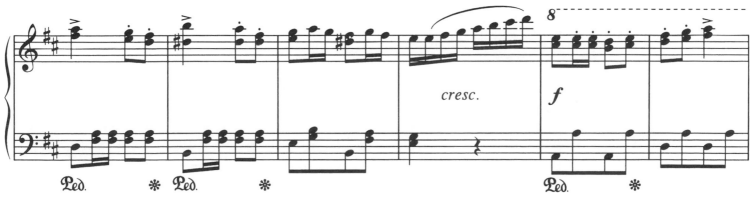

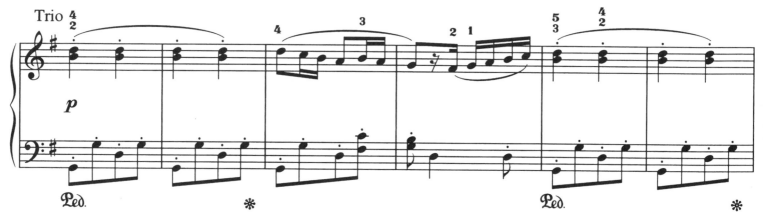

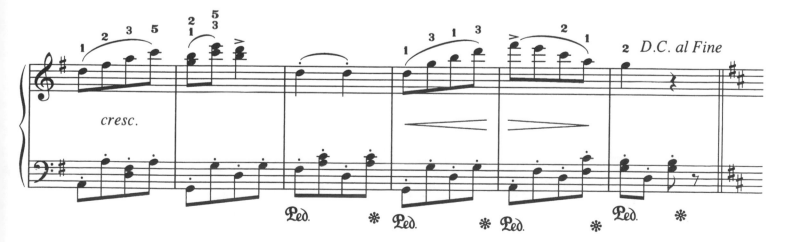

Moments Musicaux
(Op.94, D.780: No.3, 4 (excerpt) & 6)

Composed by Franz Peter Schubert

Allegro moderato

No.3

No.4
(excerpt)

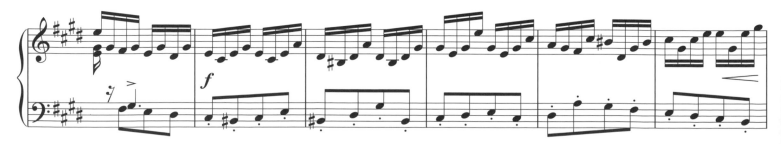

Coda ritard.

Allegretto

No.6

Trio

Allegretto D.C.

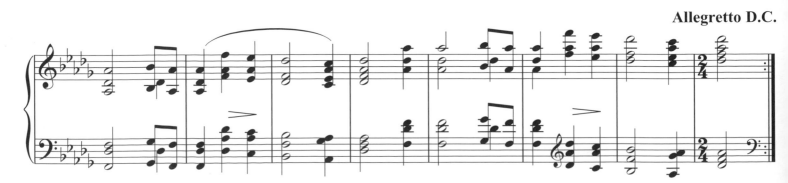

Ländler

(Op.18, D.145: No.1, 7 & 11)

Composed by Franz Peter Schubert

No.1

No.7

No.11

Nocturne in B♭ major
(Op.148: Piano Trio)

Composed by Franz Peter Schubert

Arranged by Quentin Thomas

Adagio, appassionato

con Ped.

Nacht und Träume

Composed by Franz Peter Schubert

Arranged by Quentin Thomas

Molto adagio

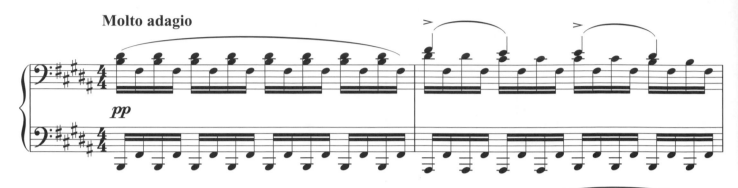

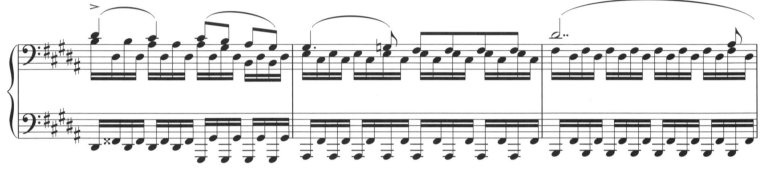

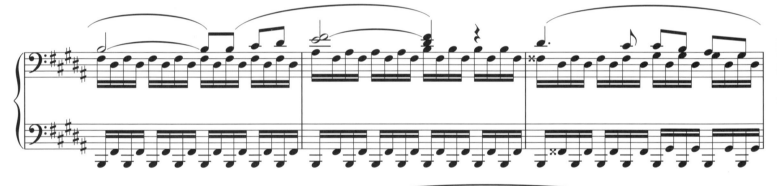

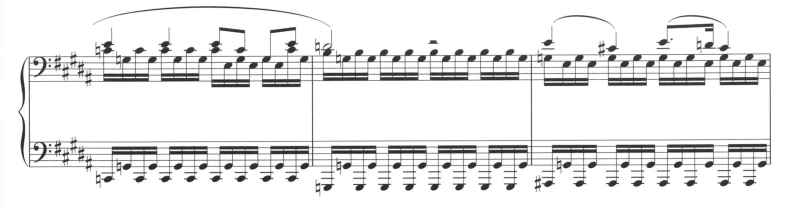

Scherzo
(D.593: No.1)

Composed by Franz Peter Schubert

Allegretto

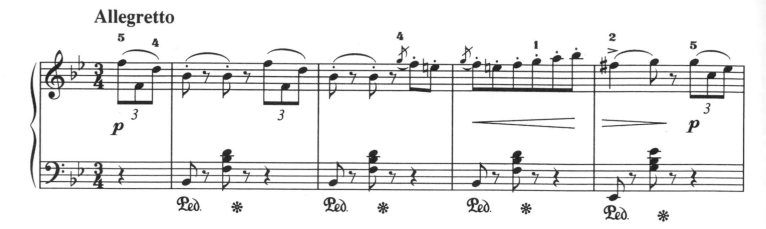

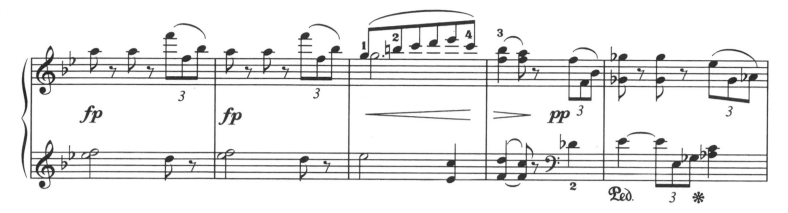

Serenade

Composed by Franz Peter Schubert

Moderato

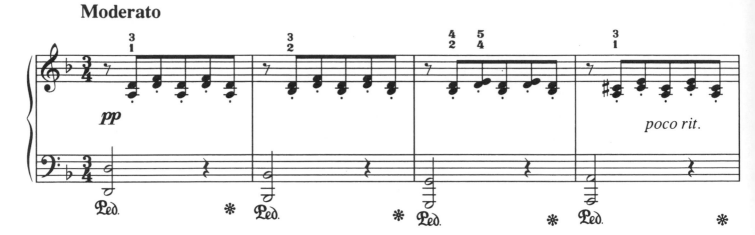

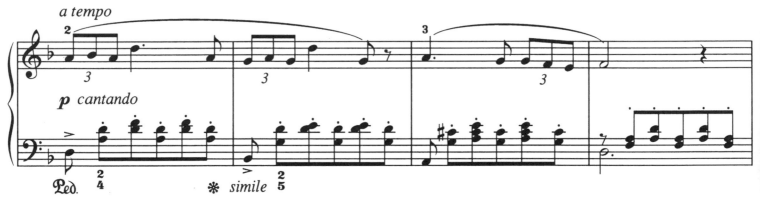

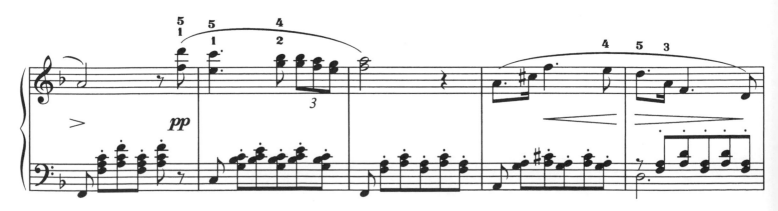

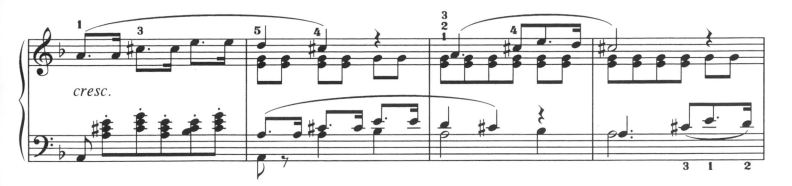

Sonata No.3
(Op.120: Andante)

Composed by Franz Peter Schubert

Andante (♩ = c.80)

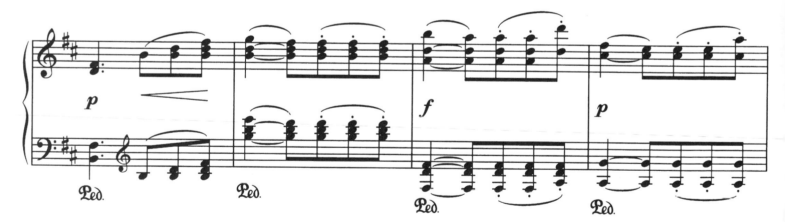

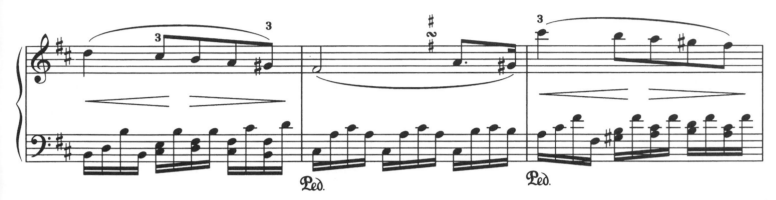

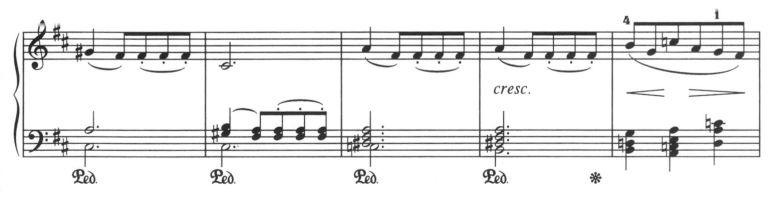

Symphony No.4 'Tragic' in C minor
(2nd movement: Andante)

Composed by Franz Peter Schubert

Arranged by Quentin Thomas

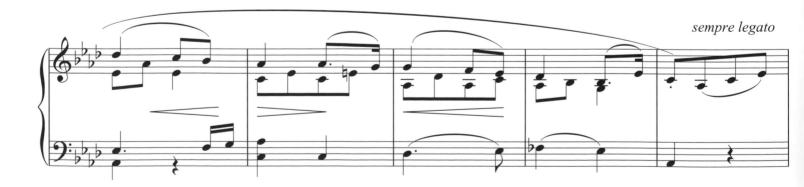

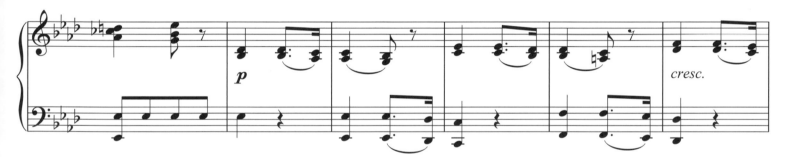

Symphony No.5 in B♭ major

(1st movement: Allegro)

Composed by Franz Peter Schubert

Arranged by Quentin Thomas

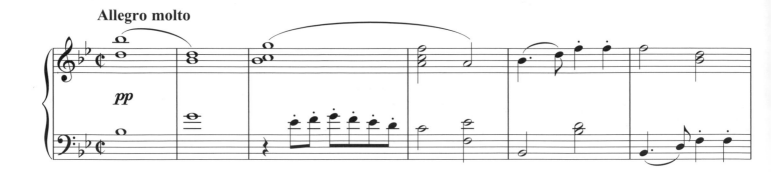

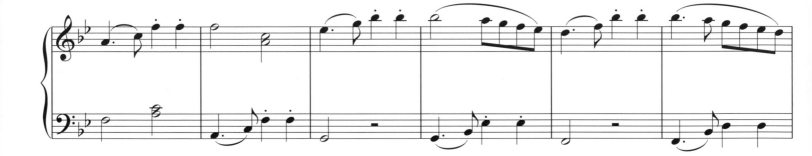

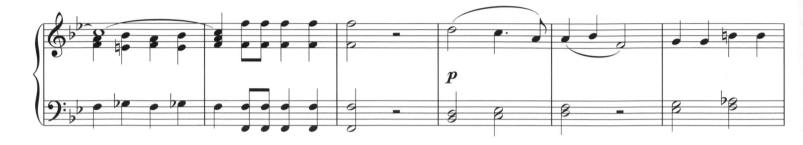

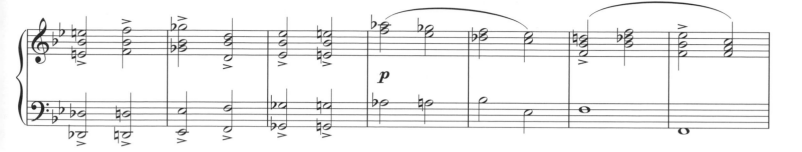

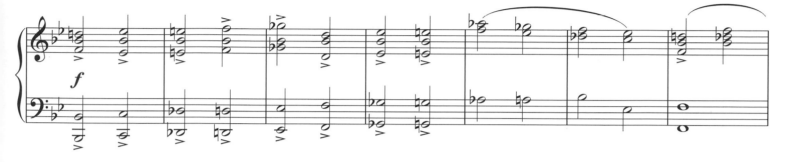

Symphony No.5 in B♭ major
(2nd movement: Andante con moto)

Composed by Franz Peter Schubert

Arranged by Quentin Thomas

Andante con moto

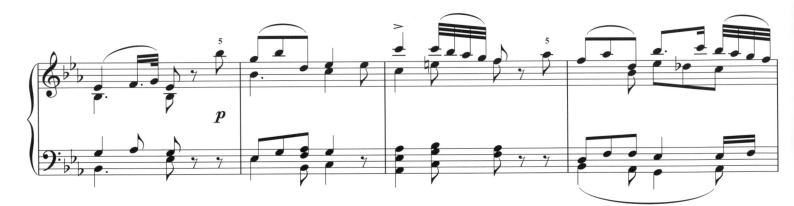

Waltz (D.844)

Composed by Franz Peter Schubert

Symphony No.5 in B♭ major

(3rd movement – Minuet: Allegro molto)

Composed by Franz Peter Schubert

Arranged by Quentin Thomas

Allegro molto

Da Capo al Fine

Symphony No.8 'Unfinished' in B minor

(2nd movement: Andante con moto)

Composed by Franz Peter Schubert

Arranged by Quentin Thomas

Andante con moto

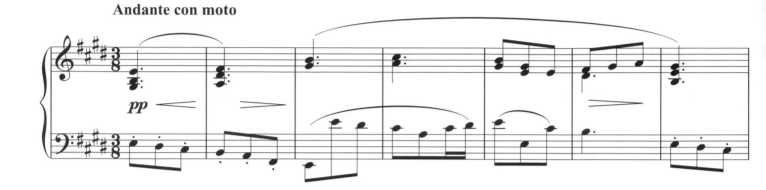

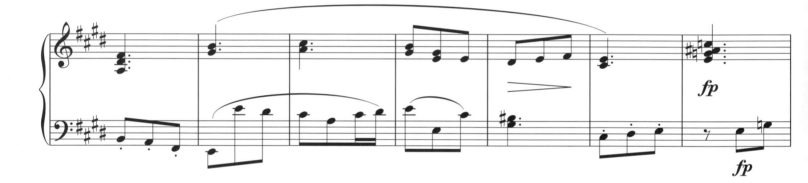

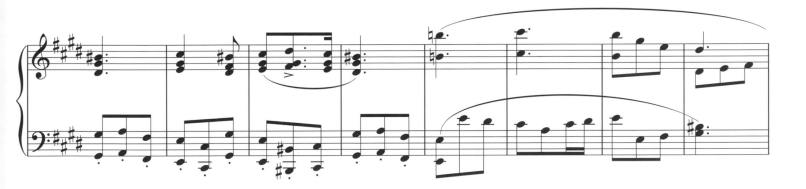

83

The Trout Quintet
(Op.114 – 4th movement: Andantino)

Composed by Franz Peter Schubert

Andantino (♩ = c.72)

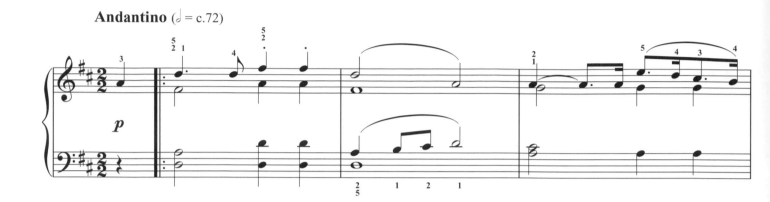

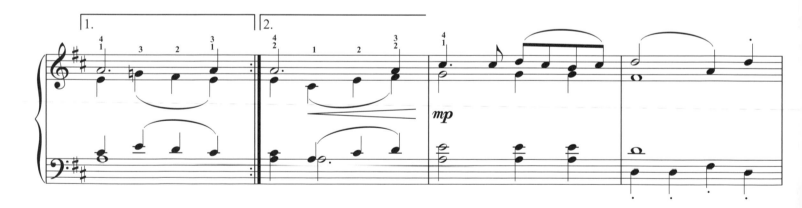

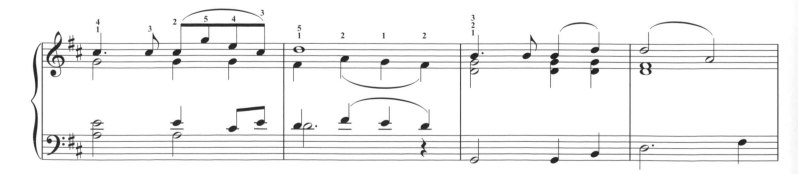

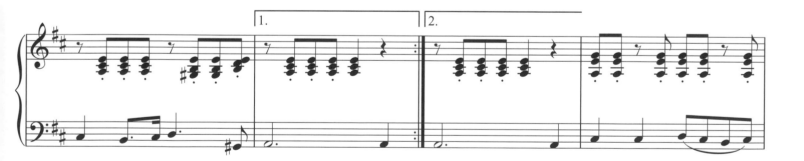

sim.

rall.

Valses Sentimentales
(Op.50, D.779: No.13, 31 & 34)
Composed by Franz Peter Schubert

No.13

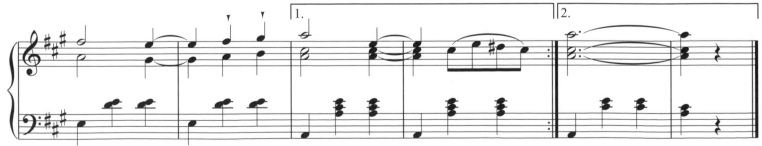

No.31

No.34

Waltzes

(Op.18, D.145: No.2 & 6)

Composed by Franz Peter Schubert

No.2

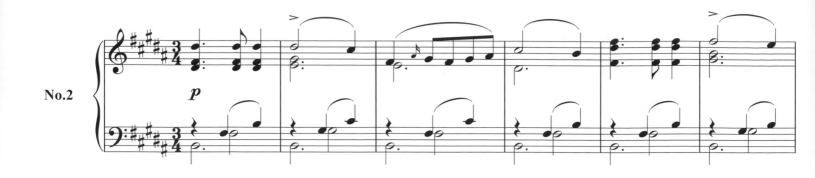

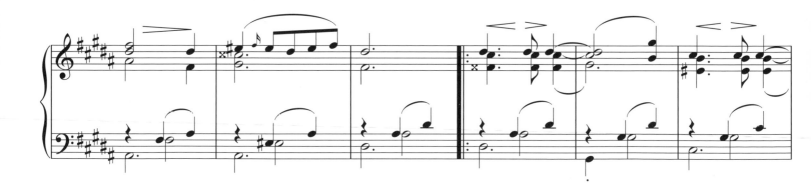

No.6

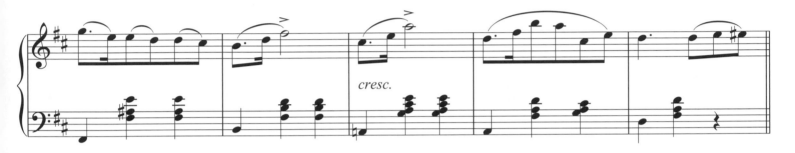

Who is Sylvia?

Composed by Franz Peter Schubert

Moderato

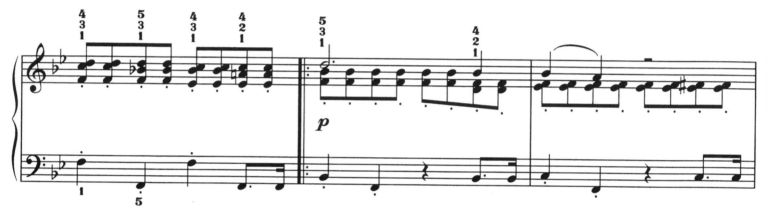

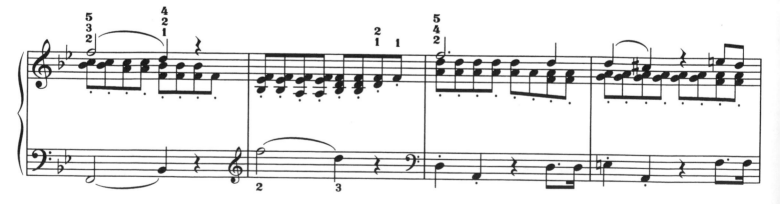

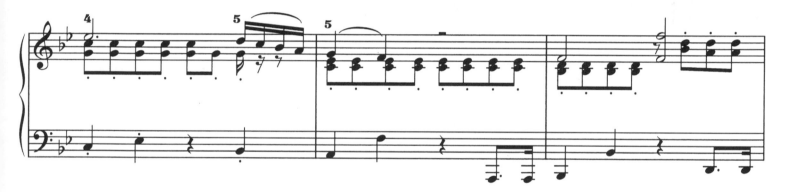

Symphony No.8 'Unfinished' in B minor
(1st movement: Allegro moderato)

Composed by Franz Peter Schubert

Allegro moderato

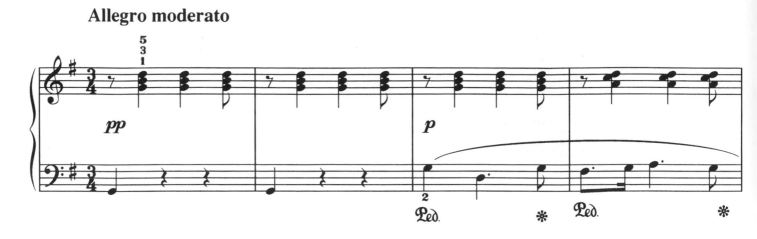

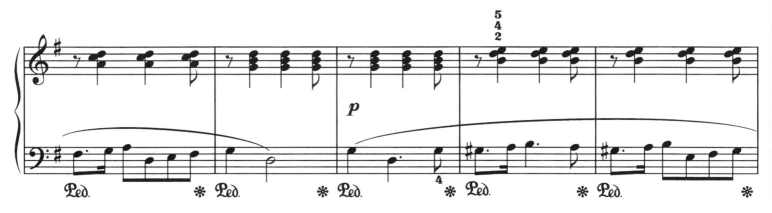

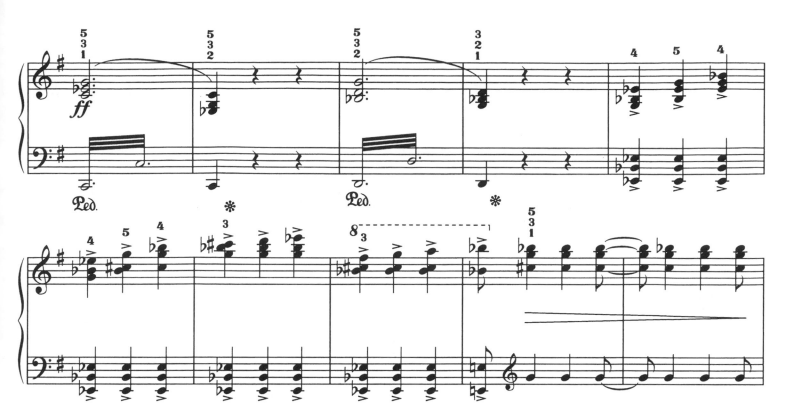

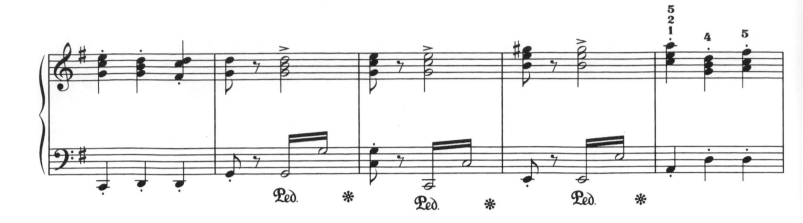

23456789